HARVEY HELLER
751 Willow Road
Lancaster, PA 17601

THE
SECOND ARK BOOK
OF RIDDLES

The Ark Book of Riddles
© 1981 David C. Cook Publishing Co.

Printed in the United States of America
ISBN 0-89191-531-1
LC: 01-68690

The Second Ark Book of Riddles

By Myra Shofner

illustrated by Dwight Walles

What meat did Noah's wife serve at every meal?

Ham.

What did the duck say when Noah gave him his lunch?

"You can put this lunch on my bill."

How do we know James, Peter, and John were left-handed?

Because they gave Paul and Barnabas their right hands in fellowship.

What did Noah say to his three sons when they went fishing off the ark?

"Take it easy, boys—
we only have two worms."

What did Noah use to tape his messages?

An ape recorder.

What advice did Noah give the fish?

"Stay in school!"

Who was the first space traveler?

Elijah. He went up in a fiery chariot.

Where could the Israelites have deposited their money?

At the banks of the Jordan.

When was Aaron like a ventriloquist?

When he spoke for his brother, Moses.

How do we know Cain took a nap when he left Eden?

He went to the land of Nod.

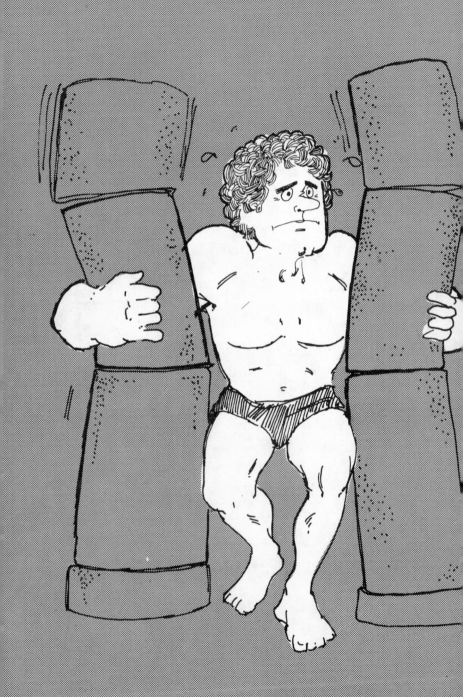

What could Samson, the strongest man who ever lived, hold for no more than a few minutes?

His breath.

How many books in the Old Testament were named after Esther?

Twenty-two. The rest were named before Esther!

Which prophets in the Bible were blind?

Ezra, Hosea, Joel, Amos, Jonah, Nahum, Habakkuk.
None of them have I's.

How was the Joseph of the Old Testament like Joseph the carpenter in the New Testament?

The first was a ruler. The second used a ruler.

How do we know the children of Israel didn't take money with them when they left Egypt?

The Book of Exodus tells us that they didn't knead (need) their dough.

Which hymn was never sung?

Bethlehem (Bethle-hymn).

What should you wear over your shirt when it's time to reap?

A harvest (har-vest).

Which rod made a hard ruler?

Herod (He-rod).

What did the smallest cow in the ark give to Noah?

Condensed milk.

What game did Adam and Eve play with God?

Hide-and-seek.

What kind of beans were in the ark?

Human beans (beings).

What person in the Bible was shorter than Zaccheus?

Job's friend, Bildad. He was a Shuhite (shoe height).

Who was even smaller?

Peter, James, and John. They went to sleep on their watch.

Why was the burial of Jacob so serious?

It was a grave subject.

What tree did Paul notice when he got to Athens?

The Idolatry (idola-tree).

Which kites were never flown?

Amalekites.

To what question could Eve never answer 'Yes'?

When Adam asked, "Have you heard this joke from anyone else, dear?"

When was Jesus an artist?

When he called Peter,
Andrew (and drew), James and John.

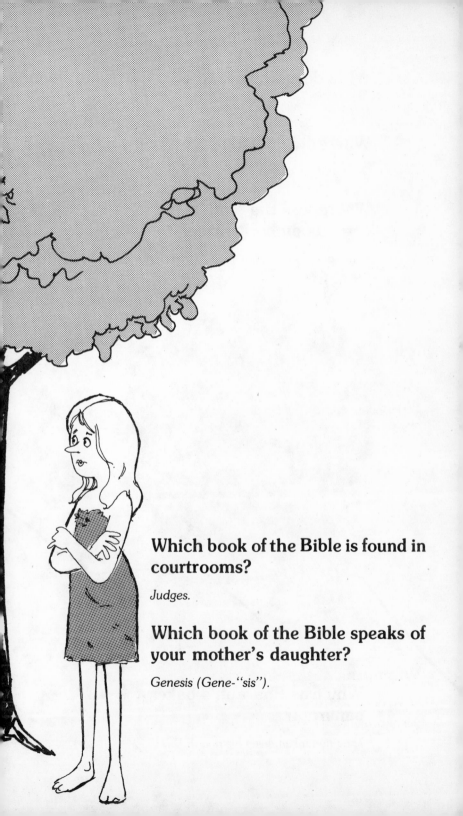

Which book of the Bible is found in courtrooms?

Judges.

Which book of the Bible speaks of your mother's daughter?

Genesis (Gene-"sis").

What does God use to keep the ocean clean?

Tide, twice a day.

Where did Samson get his hair cut?

On top of his head.

Where was the tenth commandment written?

At the bottom of the list.

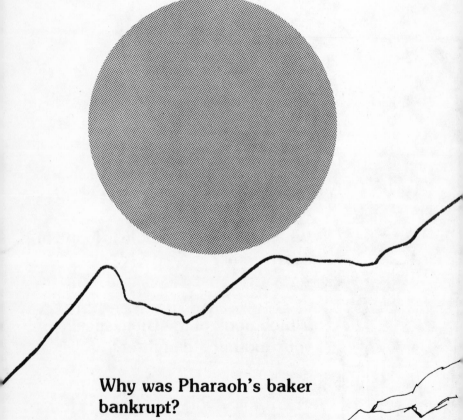

Why was Pharaoh's baker bankrupt?

They had taken away his dough.

When Moses stood on Mt. Sinai, his back was to the east, and his face was to the west. What was on his right hand?

Fingers.

What does an egg have in common with the oxen Jesus talked about?

The yoke (yolk).

Which knee was never bent?

Bethany (Betha-knee).

On which sea has no boat sailed?

Mercy (mer-sea).

Which fruits are good, but can never be eaten?

The fruits of the Spirit: love, joy, peace, patience, kindness, goodness, faithfulness, gentleness, and self-control.

Which tea does the Bible say is worthless?

Vanity (vani-tea).

What time was it when Joseph's ten brothers wanted to kill him?

Ten after one.

How long was Moses in the Wilderness?

No one knows. The Bible doesn't give his height.

What did the children of Israel have in common with modern travelers?

They had a Passover. We have an overpass.

Where did Noah keep the bees in the ark?

In the archives (ark hives).

How did Noah revive a rodent that fell overboard?

By using mouse-to-mouse resuscitation.

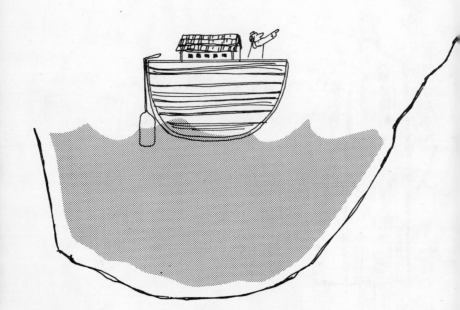

On which mountain did Noah find a rat?

On Mount Ararat (Ar-a-rat).

How were the Pharisees and Sadducees like potatoes?

Jesus said they had eyes but could not see.

What ship never sails?

Wor-ship.

Which commandment do baseball players break?

The eighth commandment. They steal bases.

Which barn was never used by a farmer?

Barn-abas.

Were there carnivals in Abraham's day?

Possibly. Sarah was a fair woman to look upon.

How do we know Abraham took all the fancy land?

Because Lot took the plain.

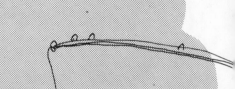

What did the reupholstered chair have in common with Peter's sick mother-in-law?

They both were recovered.

When were there ducks in the Jordan River?

When Naaman the leper took his seven ducks.

What is it that God gives away and then keeps?

His promises.

What kind of wood cannot be used in building, but makes good fishing bait?

Wormwood.

When doesn't four quarters make a dollar?

When it makes a moon.

What did they call the angry speech the umpire gave the pitcher?

The sermon on the mound.

At the creation, which weighed most, day or night?

Night, because the day was light.

HARVEY HELLER
751 Willow Road
Lancaster, PA 17601

What bird placed Jonah inside the belly of a fish?

A swallow.

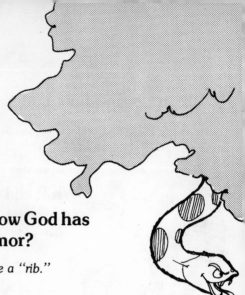

How do we know God has a sense of humor?

Because he can take a "rib."

What do we have that Adam never had?

Ancestors.

What was the first season in the Garden of Eden?

The fall.

Why was Eve's first clothing like a book?

It was made of leaves.

Did Adam and Eve walk out of the garden?

No. God drove them out.

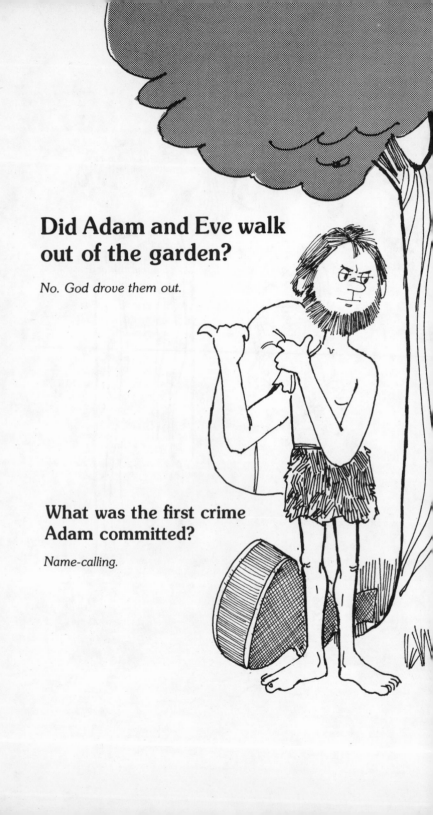

What was the first crime Adam committed?

Name-calling.

Was there a kitchen in the Garden of Eden?

Possibly. Adam and Eve wore aprons of fig leaves.

What did Adam have two of, Cain and Abel each one of, but Seth never had?

The letter A.

Why was Lot's wife's backward glance at Sodom a tragedy?

She had a Lot to lose.

Who was his own children's uncle?

Jacob. He was uncle to Leah's children by his marriage to her sister Rachel and vice versa.

What furniture did Moses take down with him from Mt. Sinai?

Tables of stone.

What did the lions in the lions' den do when God closed their mouths?

They took a yap nap.

Which automobile is named in the Bible?

Sychar (si-car).

What days in the Bible passed most rapidly?

The FAST days.

In what room of the Persian king's house did Daniel spend the night?

In the den.

Who ate the world's mos

Esau. It cost him his birthright.

xpensive meal?

What did Solomon build in Jerusalem that each person has two of?

A temple.

What was the first math problem ever worked?

When God divided the light from the darkness.

What first two rulers on earth can still be seen today?

The sun, which ruled the day, and the moon, which ruled the night.

Why did Moses go to Mt. Sinai?

Because Mt. Sinai wouldn't come to Moses.

How was Dorcas, the good woman of Joppa, like a farmer?

She gathered and sewed. A farmer sews and gathers.

What was the difference between the 10,000 soldiers of Israel and the 300 soldiers Gideon chose for battle?

9,700.

How do we know Peter was a rich fisherman?

By his net income.

What king had a tight hold?

Agrippa (A-grip-pa).

How did Saul feel after his name was changed?

Appalled (aPauled).

What battle was won with a single blow?

The battle of Jericho.

Whose hair became a real hang-up?

Absalom's, when he hung from a tree.

When is wine like a mathematician?

Proverbs says wine bites like an adder.

What Bible city will fit on an automobile?

Tyre (tire).

How did Mary show that Jesus was a gift to the world?

She wrapped him.

What baseball term is found in Genesis?

It speaks of the big inning (beginning).

When was the first face washed?

When the mist watered the face of the earth.

What drink was in the pot the Samaritan woman brought to the well?

There was "t" (tea) in the pot.

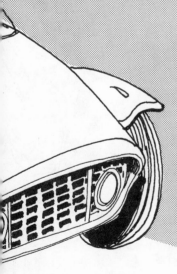

Who paid the highest price ever paid for a haircut?

Samson. It cost him his strength and his eyesight.

Why did the paralyzed man who was brought to Jesus feel sad?

His four friends let him down.

What was the first recorded robbery?

The time Aaron and Hur "held up" the arms of Moses.

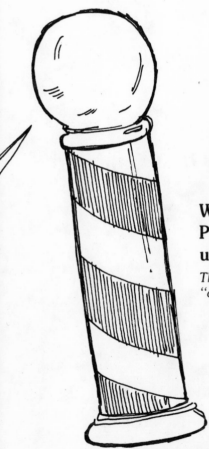

Which relative does Proverbs tell us to be like?

The ant (aunt). We are to "consider her ways" and be wise.

Who had the first tailored clothes?

Adam and Eve. God made them coats of skin.

What do you have that Cain and Abel never had?

Grandparents.

What household chore would Adam feel a kinship for?

Dusting. He was made from dust.

How was the prune like Joseph?

The pit is in one, and the other was in the pit.

Who was the last man in the world Samson wanted to see?

A barber.

What sport did Jacob engage in?

He wrestled with an angel.

What baseball player did Rebekah know?

The pitcher that she brought to the well.

What belt never held up any pants?

Belteshazzar (Belt-eshazzar), the Babylonian king.

What musical instrument of King David's was dishonest?

The lyre.

Which of David's wives spelled bad weather?

Abigail (Abi-gail).

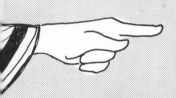

What insect went to Egypt on a donkey?

The flea. The angel told Joseph to take Mary, the baby Jesus, and flee (flea) into Egypt.

How old were the goats when Adam named them?

They were only kids.

What could Adam never say to his young sons?

"When I was your age . . ."

Who brought something to Paul with which to write?

Priscilla. She brought Aquila (a-quill-a).

How do we know Paul wanted everyone to get a good education?

He said, "I would not have you ignorant, brothers!"

What did both Abraham and the suffocating man want?

The heir (air).

Why did the unemployed man get excited when he was looking through his Bible?

He thought he saw a Job.

When were the first musical groups formed?

By Jacob, when he divided his people, possessions, and animals into two bands.

How were Joseph and Zaccheus alike?

*Joseph's job was **overseeing**, and Zaccheus's problem was **seeing over.***

**Who was sick
at the battle of Ai?**

*Carmi's son, but of course
he was always Achan (achin').*

Who kept the people laughing?

The king of Amalek. He was a Agag (a gag).